► YouTubers

EMMA
CHAMBERLAIN

JESSICA RUSICK

**Checkerboard
Library**

An Imprint of Abdo Publishing
abdobooks.com

abdobooks.com

Published by Abdo Publishing, a division of ABDO, PO Box 398166, Minneapolis, Minnesota 55439. Copyright © 2020 by Abdo Consulting Group, Inc. International copyrights reserved in all countries. No part of this book may be reproduced in any form without written permission from the publisher. Checkerboard Library™ is a trademark and logo of Abdo Publishing.

Printed in the United States of America, North Mankato, Minnesota
102019
012020

THIS BOOK CONTAINS
RECYCLED MATERIALS

Design: Sarah DeYoung, Mighty Media, Inc.
Production: Mighty Media, Inc.
Editor: Rebecca Felix
Cover Photograph: Laurent Zabulon/Abaca/Sipa USA/AP Images
Interior Photographs: Abaca Press/AP Images, pp. 27, 29 (top); David Livingston/Getty Images, p. 19; Mighty Media, Inc., pp. 21, 25 (left, right); Nicholas Hunt/Getty Images, p. 15; Rich Polk/Getty Images, p. 5; Shutterstock Images, pp. 7, 9, 13, 17, 24, 28; Stefanie Keenan/Getty Images, pp. 11, 23, 29 (bottom); Tess_Trunk/iStockphoto, pp. 16, 18, 22, 24, 25, 28, 29

Library of Congress Control Number: 2019943214

Publisher's Cataloging-in-Publication Data
Names: Rusick, Jessica, author.
Title: Emma Chamberlain / by Jessica Rusick
Description: Minneapolis, Minnesota : Abdo Publishing, 2020 | Series: YouTubers | Includes online resources and index.
Identifiers: ISBN 9781532191787 (lib. bdg.) | ISBN 9781644943564 (pbk.) | ISBN 9781532178511 (ebook)
Subjects: LCSH: Chamberlain, Emma--Juvenile literature. | YouTube (Firm)--Juvenile literature. | Internet celebrities--Biography--Juvenile literature. | Video blogs--Juvenile literature. | Internet videos--Juvenile literature. | Internet entertainment industry--Juvenile literature.
Classification: DDC 646.7092--dc23

Contents

Emma Chamberlain

Emma Chamberlain is a social media star. She is known for her YouTube channel named after herself. Chamberlain started her channel in 2017. Since then, she has gained more than 8 million **subscribers**. Her videos have been viewed more than 750 million times!

In Chamberlain's videos, she talks directly to the camera. She narrates her daily life in a funny and **unscripted** way. Chamberlain is known for her **sarcastic** sense of humor and video editing. She uses cuts, zooms, and sound effects to add humor to her videos.

Chamberlain is also known for her fashion sense and certain items she loves. Fans admire her casual style. And they associate her with the iced coffee she drinks and lip balm she uses in most of her videos.

Fans relate to Chamberlain and her daily life experiences. Her personality shined from a young age. But Chamberlain also faced struggles on her way to stardom.

Emma Chamberlain won the 2018 Streamy Award for Breakout Creator. The Streamy Awards honor the top content creators in social media.

Humble Beginnings

Emma Chamberlain was born on May 22, 2001, in a **suburb** of Silicon Valley, California. Emma doesn't share her mother's name on social media. But she does share information about her father. His name is Michael, and he is an artist.

Emma's childhood was not always easy. Her parents divorced when she was young. Emma lived with her mom in a small apartment. Money was often a struggle.

Then, Emma's father got sick and was unable to work. So, money became a greater concern for Emma's family during this time. Emma's dad eventually recovered. But Emma never forgot how scary it felt to worry about his health.

Despite her family's struggles, Emma was known as a fun and outgoing person. She was always making people laugh. Emma didn't know what type of career she wanted in the future. But she had a sense that she would use her personality to get there.

The Silicon Valley suburb where Emma grew up is in Northern California, near the coast.

In 2015, Emma began attending Notre Dame High School in Belmont, California. She was a cheerleader there. Emma edited video clips of her team's performances. Later, she would use these editing skills to get through a tough time.

Online Interest

As a sophomore in high school, Emma felt stressed and unhappy. She was overwhelmed with homework. This made it feel difficult to show up to class. When Emma did attend class, she struggled to pay attention.

For most of her life, Emma had put great effort into school. She felt she had to get good grades to build a successful future. But now, Emma wondered if traditional school was the right fit for her.

At the end of her sophomore year, Emma's mental health worsened. After failing a driving test, she fell into a **depression**. She stopped going to school and seeing her friends. Emma said this was one of the worst times of her life.

In May 2017, Emma asked her father for help. She wanted to find a positive way to get through this hard time. After their conversation, Emma decided to start a YouTube channel. She had always loved to watch YouTube videos and felt starting a channel could lift her spirits.

Emma started watching YouTube videos when she was six years old.

First Footage

Emma posted her first video to YouTube on June 2, 2017. She had filmed the video in San Francisco, California, with her father.

The video is different from Emma's later, **typical** videos where she speaks directly to the camera. In this video, Emma speaks only during an introduction. Then she poses silently, showing off outfits she put together.

In coming days, Emma posted more videos. She saw that DIY videos were popular on YouTube. So, she thought she should make one too. Emma's DIY video shows viewers how to decorate shoes with iron-on patches.

But DIY did not feel right to Emma. In a 2018 interview she said, "I don't know how to do crafts! I don't know what I was thinking." So, Emma went in a different direction. On June 7, she posted her first **vlog**.

Emma appears reserved and formal in her first two videos. In them, she wears makeup and speaks in a practiced way.

Emma films at an event. For much of her early YouTube career, Emma filmed her vlogs using an iPhone. Later, she switched to a camera.

Emma appears much more casual in her first **vlog**. She wears no makeup and her hair is in a messy bun. She speaks in an **unscripted** way. The video also showcases her **sarcastic** sense of humor.

The vlog follows Emma's quest to find a fidget spinner. These toys became wildly popular in 2017. In the video, Emma jokes about missing out on this craze. After she buys a fidget spinner, she says it's nothing special. But the rest of the video shows Emma secretly using the toy in her everyday life.

Emma used her editing skills to add humor to the fidget spinner video. These included quick cuts, unexpected zooms, and sound effects. These would become part of Emma's **signature** content style.

Emma said at the end of her first vlog that she had fun making it. So, she made more! In her vlogs, Emma continued to narrate her daily life. She discussed the weather, foods she ate, and more.

Emma's fanbase grew quickly. By mid-July, she had about 1,000 **subscribers**. Soon, a **viral** video would launch Emma into YouTube fame.

In Emma's fidget spinner video, she uses the toy while driving, at the gym, cooking, and more.

Viral Video

In early July 2017, Emma's **subscriber** count was growing steadily. A video she posted at the end of that month would cause it to soar.

On July 27, Emma posted "We All Owe the Dollar Store an Apology." In this video, Emma shows off items she bought at the dollar store. This includes a scarf, candy, and more. Emma uses **sarcasm** to make fun of the products. She also uses quick cuts and other edits to add humor to the video.

This video was not much different from Emma's earlier **vlogs**. But this video went **viral**. One month after posting the dollar store video, Emma had gained more than 100,000 new subscribers! The post remained popular for years. By 2019, it had more than 4 million views.

Emma's videos had officially found a following. But Emma was not concerned with subscriber counts. She posted on YouTube because it made her happy.

Emma's viral video shot her into stardom. Soon after, Emma was featured in several magazine articles and photo shoots.

Posting also made Emma feel like she had some control over her **depression**. But as summer neared its end, returning to school weighed on her mind.

School Struggles

By August, Emma was in a better place mentally. But returning to school that month brought her stress. Emma thought **vlogging** while at school might make her feel better. She filmed herself saying funny things in class and with friends.

These videos did make Emma feel better while at school. And the school vlogs were popular with her **subscribers**. But vlogging in school was against the rules. School officials told Chamberlain she had to stop.

VIP Post

In October 2017, Emma posted "Why I Left School." In this video, she talks about her school struggles. In 2019, the video had received more than 7 million views.

So, Emma began vlogging after school. But this was also her time to do homework. Sometimes Emma stayed up all night to make time for both. The late nights increased her stress.

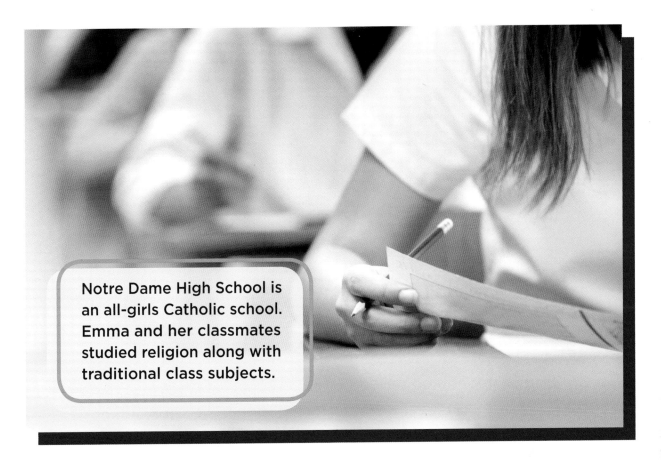

Notre Dame High School is an all-girls Catholic school. Emma and her classmates studied religion along with traditional class subjects.

School felt too overwhelming for Emma. She felt she had to leave school for her mental health. She talked to her parents. In September 2017, they agreed to let Emma leave school.

But Emma still wanted to graduate. So in 2018, she took and passed the California High School Exit Exam. This test let her graduate high school early. With high school behind her, Emma was ready to devote more time to YouTube.

The Emma Chamberlain Effect

Emma's online success grew. In April 2018 she reached 1 million YouTube **subscribers**! Emma posted a video thanking her fans for the milestone.

Part of Emma's success was due to her fans. Many of her fans are from a generation called Gen Z. These are people born after 1996. Gen Z viewers are more likely to watch YouTube videos and look up to YouTube stars. Gen Z viewers are also more likely to become fans of people they feel are **genuine**.

Fans believed Emma was genuine. Many of her videos focus on her doing

Because the tone of Emma's content is casual and relaxed, some viewers think her videos are easy to make. But Emma said she can spend more than 30 hours editing each one!

Emma has helped bring back the popularity of scrunchies. These cloth hair accessories were first created in the 1980s.

common, everyday activities. Some **critics** have called this type of content boring. But Emma's fans related to her seemingly ordinary teenage lifestyle. They also related to her humor.

Emma was known for her **sarcasm** and **self-deprecating** humor. She often recorded herself reacting to her videos as she edited them. During these reactions, Emma **typically** made fun of herself for things she did in the edited videos.

Emma added her reactions while editing to her finished videos. Gen Z viewers liked this style of humor. They appreciated stars who were able to poke fun at themselves.

Fans also admired Emma's casual fashion sense. Emma often wore oversized sweatshirts and a scrunchie in her hair. These elements of Emma's style became part of her **persona**.

Emma's habits also became well-known by her fans. She often sipped iced coffee in her videos. Emma also frequently mentioned and used lip balm. Together, these things became part of her persona too.

As Emma's popularity grew, some fans began to dress, talk, and act like her. Media outlets called this the "Emma Chamberlain Effect." Emma had become an influencer.

Influencers are social media stars with large fanbases. Companies pay influencers to promote brands. This is called brand sponsorship. Emma's fans related to her and trusted her. So, they were more likely to buy brands she used or mentioned.

In May 2018, Emma got a brand sponsorship from the skincare company Curology. It paid her to promote its brand in a video. More **collaborations** were just around the corner for Emma.

Emma sells a T-shirt showing her as a mythical creature called a centaur and drinking her signature iced coffee.

Sister Squad

Emma continued to earn fans. By June 2018, her **subscribers** grew to more than 2 million! That same month, Emma moved to Los Angeles, California. She wanted to be closer to opportunities in the entertainment industry.

One opportunity was **collaborations** with other social media stars. As Emma's fame took off, James Charles contacted her. James was a fellow YouTuber and Los Angeles resident. His beauty **vlogging** channel had millions of subscribers.

James gave Emma advice about living in the city. Soon after moving, Emma met James in person. The two became friends. Then James introduced Emma to YouTube stars and twin brothers Grayson and Ethan Dolan. Together, Emma and her new friends called themselves the Sister Squad.

In 2019, it was rumored that Chamberlain was dating Sister Squad member Ethan Dolan.   Neither star commented on this rumor.

The Dolan Twins have a popular YouTube channel. But they got their start on the video-sharing app Vine in 2013.

The Sister Squad filmed videos together. Then they posted the videos to their individual channels. In the squad's first video, Emma received a makeover from James and the Dolan Twins. The video became one of Emma's most popular posts. In 2019, it had more than 19 million views!

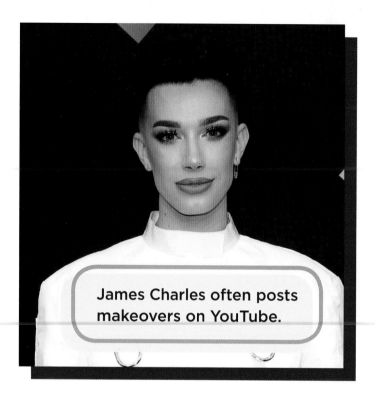

James Charles often posts makeovers on YouTube.

VIP Post

In August 2018, the Sister Squad filmed themselves on a road trip to Las Vegas, Nevada. This video became Emma's most popular ever. One year later it had more than 27 million views!

The Sister Squad was a success. The friends made more videos. They filmed themselves giving one another gifts, vacationing together, and more.

New Channels

Clothing & Accessories: Chamberlain sells a clothing line called High Key on the shopping app Dote. It includes scrunchies, tank tops, a denim jacket, a fuzzy jacket, and more. Chamberlain also sells **merchandise** on her personal website. These items include hoodies, T-shirts, and hats.

Podcast: Chamberlain launched a 2019 **podcast** called Stupid Genius. In its episodes, Chamberlain poses questions and then tries to guess the answers.

Making friends with fellow YouTube stars helped Emma adjust to living in Los Angeles. She said the squad members were some of the best friends she'd ever had.

Emma's Sister Squad **collaboration** also earned her more fans very quickly. Just one month after moving to Los Angeles, her **subscriber** count rose by another 1 million. Emma now had more than 3 million people subscribing to her YouTube videos. On average, another 200,000 subscribed each week.

Fashion & Future

As Chamberlain's content expanded, so did her platforms. In August 2018, she **debuted** a clothing line called High Key on the shopping app Dote. The line included scrunchies, clothing, and more. But there was a catch.

Chamberlain offered a High Key presale in July. In this presale, she blurred images of the items. Fans could not see what High Key items looked like. Even so, the line sold out in just two hours during the presale!

That November, Chamberlain debuted clothing and **merchandise** on her personal website. These items featured imagery of Chamberlain.

Chamberlain's products were a hit with her growing fanbase. By summer 2019, she had more than 8 million **subscribers**. And she was gaining fans on another platform too.

In April, Chamberlain launched a **podcast** called Stupid Genius. In each episode, she explores such questions as "Why Do Dogs Lick Humans?"

Chamberlain isn't sure what she will try next. But her plan is simple. She said, "My goal in the future is honestly just to be happy. That's it. I try to live in the moment."

Chamberlain became better known for her fashion after launching a clothing line. She has since attended several fashion events, where photographers capture her style.

Timeline

2001

Emma Chamberlain is born on May 22 in a suburb of Silicon Valley, California.

2017

In June, Chamberlain posts her first YouTube video.

2017

Chamberlain leaves school in September.

2015

Chamberlain begins attending Notre Dame High School in Belmont, California.

2017

Chamberlain posts "Why We All Owe the Dollar Store an Apology" in July. It is her first viral video.

2018

In April, Chamberlain's YouTube channel reaches 1 million subscribers.

2018

Chamberlain gets a brand sponsorship from skincare company Curology in May.

2018

In July, Chamberlain's channel reaches more than 3 million subscribers.

2018

Chamberlain debuts a merchandise line on her personal website in November.

2018

Chamberlain posts her first collaboration with the Sister Squad in June.

2018

In July, a presale of Chamberlain's clothing line, High Key, sells out in two hours.

2019

Chamberlain launches the podcast Stupid Genius. Her subscriber count on YouTube rises to 8 million.

Glossary

collaboration—the act of working with another person or group in order to do something or reach a goal.

critic—a professional who gives his or her opinion on art, literature, or performances.

debut (DAY-byoo)—to present or perform something for the first time.

depression—a state of feeling sad or dejected.

genuine—honest and sincere.

merchandise—goods that are bought and sold.

persona—the personality someone presents in public.

podcast—an audio program made available for download over the Internet.

sarcasm—a sharp, mocking form of humor. Someone who uses sarcasm is sarcastic.

self-deprecating—critical of oneself in a humorous way.

signature—something that sets apart or identifies an individual, group, or company.

subscriber—someone who signs up to receive something on a regular basis.

suburb—a town, village, or community just outside a city.

typical—usual or normal.

unscripted—not following prepared written words.

viral—quickly or widely spread, usually by electronic communication.

vlog—a video log that tells about someone's personal opinions, activities, and experiences.

Online Resources

Index